Unburdened Kisses

Also by Toni Thomas:

Chosen
> Brick Road Poetry Press

Fast as Lightening
> Gribble Press

Walking on Water
> Finishing Line Press

Blue Halo
> Annalese Press

Ace Raider of the Unfathomable Universe
> Annalese Press

You'll be Fast as Lightning Coveting my Painted Tail
> Annalese Press

Hotsy Totsy Ballroom
> Annalese Press

Love Adrift in the City of Stars
> Annalese Press

In the Pink Arms of the City
> Annalese Press

In the Kingdom of Longing
> Annalese Press

The Things We Don't Know
> Annalese Press

In the Boarding House for Unclaimed Girls
> Annalese Press

They Became Wing Perfect and Flew
> Annalese Press

Unburdened Kisses

Poems

First published in 2022 by
Annalese Press
134 Towngate
Netherthong
Holmfirth
West Yorkshire HD9 3XZ
England

Copyright © 2022 Toni Thomas

Please Note:
All characters and situations appearing
in these pages are in the service of poetry.
Any resemblance to real persons,
living or dead, is purely coincidental.

All rights reserved. No part of this publication may be reproduced, stored, or transmitted in any form, or by any means electronic, mechanical or photocopying, recording or otherwise, without the express written permission of the publisher.

Elvira resting at a Table by Amedeo Modigliani
St Louis Art Museum, PD-US
Cover design and sketches by Peter Wadsworth

British Library Cataloguing-in-Publication Data
A catalogue record for this book is available on request from the British Library.

ISBN 978-1-9163620-7-9

Contents

Part One: *Stir Crazy for Hot Dates*

You stamp across the cobbles	3
It is May	4
We are stir crazy for hot dates	5
I want to be red sauce	6
You drive like a banshee	7
I burrow a hole	8
Sometimes the world barely fits	9
I am trying to decipher	10
In the dream you run a hostel	11
In the dowry of my heart	12
Last night the moon bled	13

Part Two: *Unnoticed Galaxies*

Some days are an emptied river	17
Not all things incriminate	18
Sunday mornings we grill pancakes	19
The postulate morning	21
On Sundays	22
In August	23
You go around	24
Happiness called	25
The Houdini of Cramped Space	26
It is auction time	27

Part Three: *Windfall*

There are seasons	31
You deal in rice and ringlets	32
We cracked the egg	33
Some years are broken toys	34
You lean over my morning	35
We are pouring syrup	36
Before wind generators	37
We came slow	39
The whirligig couldn't hold us	40
We couldn't stare you down	41
To praise the dark	42
Who says we are impermeable	43
I call you Inspector Caruso	44
Who calls the bird out of hiding	45
Our neighbors are round and poor	46
You speak in parables	47

Part Four: *We are Stargazing*

The playground of the dark	51
When I tap terrestrial	52
We came here to play	53
We scoop up fantasy	54
We talk about bright wings	55
I am fingering the fanciful	56
I crumple paper	57
In the soft hollow	58
This morning	59
The bandoneon kept saying	60
We are playing Parcheesi	61
You want me to kiss and tell	62
The silhouette of the moon	63
We are peeling oranges	64

You have bride groomed for a day	65
I took you home last night	66
You hold no peephole	67
What if our bodies	68

PART FIVE: *Liquid Kisses*

You wander my body	73
You are inventive	74
Every day I let you wander	75
Everything seduces me	76
In the right light	77
It is the season	78
Some lovers stay with us	79
I vow by midnight	80
It is good to remember	81
It is early June	82
On Bastille Day	83
You are eating kippers	84
In the thorn bush	85
I could promise you	86
The day is heavy with the scent of sedge	87
You rattle the stars	88
In the script of your world	89
I map my hands	90
We sing morning star and hope	91
I sew on wings	92

Your voice is wild and simple.
You are untranslatable
Into any one tongue.

Anna Akhmatova

There was a time when people used to walk around singing

Toni Morrison

Part One

Stir Crazy for Hot Dates

You stamp across the cobbles

in your provocative
that never runs dry
commits adultery

is more than seersucker cute
a tempting éclair.

Some fantasies get stolen
some preserve in aspic
some are a slut hotel
blue haven.

When you say – *take me*
you don't say it lightly
not like skin peeling
the removal of stretch marks

talk about the whole thing
warts and cankers
yellow chiffon and a burning bush

tepid not being an accurate
vocabulary for love.

It is May

time of corsages, a prom dress
when some marriages sport blossom
ivory as snow
others wither to death pitiless.
The moon gets canonized
the azalea want to feel more than
monumental.

I learn to mythologize fear
wear my occupations brightly
mortar the sun
shave down my legs
parody want into a slush cone.

See how I slit the dark down its veins
squeeze you into my bathrobe
grind words
press them into an irresistible homily.

We are stir crazy for hot dates

colored wings
tater tots, caramel ice cream
melon slices that slush

stir crazy for balconied midnight
skinny dips and ring toss
a marbled future
movable chairs and kiss kiss

for starfish and goulash
Goodwill castoffs
the patio deck with tiki lights, salsa

want more than the bruised ocean
fantasy bungalow
voice gone knife blade

watch you crowbar my past
man handle the snow
impervious.

I want to be red sauce

ooze onto your plate
with my chunks of tomato
onion, garlic, hint of Sicily

want to mount the moon
swim naked
swear at the dark
for not hosting

am junkets of slush
a twinkle lit deck
underneath the hidden
jolt of sour candy

brush my teeth
twenty swipes
for a pearly future
paste back the bent
arm of roses.

You drive like a banshee

few folks will stake their life
to the sobriety of your wheels

but then maybe the world has
always been hell-bent
pinned to the next curve
caution taped to no one.

I have seen you swerve off the road
climb back up
slug whiskey
while you contemplate Armageddon

steer toward the coast
slide your wheels over the divide
as if with your souped up stereo
fast hand on the gears
you have something special to say.

I burrow a hole

call it rabbit shelter
repository
loot box
underground kisses
in case the god of cruelty arrives

have burrowed many holes
to keep the rabbit family happy
my treasure guarded
vested them with mulch
scraps of lace
the imprisoned prom dress
forgotten pedigree.

Sometimes the world speaks gnarly
families dissolve
children erupt
the dark carries a singed suitcase.

I burrow a hole
so I can sleep right
don't call it *insurance policy*
a metal safe for the rich
don't stir the blind
with a birch stick
poke the night's orphaned hurt
with my heels.

Sometimes the world barely fits

I sit in a box marked *winter*
sermons don't pierce
the mathematics of hope
settles for a bread roll.

At moments like this it is good
to remember less tyrant places
where sunset leaks

Englicio Sanchez
wore my body
to beautiful ruin
with a single kiss.

I am trying to decipher

the good from the dark
true lover from mock trial
place my suitcase
voice somewhere

understand winter
the man pacing the floor
with his pistol
our marginalized snow scene
stripped down manger

why the girl in the blue coat
who refuses to sodomize winter
is destined to turn blind.

In the dream you run a hostel

with fortune tellers
a pampered river.
It holds margins of light
a summer awning
men who dress smart
underneath are shy boys.
Your mouth is pearled
offers a way home.

In the dream I wear chiffon
rose crystal
serve cocktails
scrap the dust off
ensure mornings aren't awkward.

Nobody sucks blood
porcelains the sky
arrives in a room with no view.

I offer up saffron
red potato, fish
marry my life to your
wet siren of kisses.

In the dowry of my heart

a pole star burns
bright as a secret corridor
carries my abandoned wishes
the girl gathering mint by the river.

She stays ripe with an April
nobody owns.

In the dowry of my heart
there are fetes and nosegays
a bass player
children forage the dark
sip the clouds empty

I know how to court flame
cup your gaze
turn my mouth
meadow.

Last night the moon bled

no pollyanna
someone drank quinine
murdered their wife

you fetched a bucket
water from the well
brought bread to the table

children fawned over you

every plate of sardines
swam in oil
translucent as death.

PART TWO

Unnoticed Galaxies

Some days are an emptied river

thoughts of you stay
hitched to my sweater
the way you move
stall at the window
spread trays of seed
suet.

Some days I watch you eat
the scraps that are given
tuck faith into your porridge.

Disabused of our troll nets
pilfered cargo
do you wait for the fog to clear
so that slow
you can slip down the cobbled street
past the clapboard houses
gutted fish

the memories, hope of me
back into the perilous
that for you is just ocean?

Not all things incriminate

are showy
the past's peep show
or held in limbo
in case a better season arrives.

I have seen discarded women
refuse an end game
crippled men learn to walk
tenements spawn a new face

have seen the boy up the road
deliver fish
even as his hands ache
the black cat come back
remember the glint
of your milk bowl
birds arrive
out of the shambles of winter
undeterred.

Sunday morning we grill pancakes

watch the child couple on the windowsill
bob, slide in close
when the sun finds them.
They are shy, attentive
light a slow campfire under their bed
as we flip our cakes
spoon more batter into the fry pan
watch.

I like that the girl's clothes are simple
pleated skirt, round collared top.
She has copper hair in a blunt cut, soft eyes.
His hair is sandy, cheeks flushed.

My daughter guesses they have known
each other for a long time
come from adjacent villages
says he has sheepherder hands
the girl works with colored thread
dreams a box garden, animals, children.
They both like buttered crumpets
he can pull trout out of the river
with his bare hands.
She knows how to be thankful.

It is rhythmic to eat pancakes while
they move in close, kiss
pool the maple syrup onto our plates

hear the *click click click* of their heads
bobbing in sunlight
the sponge of their joined lips
smooch smooch smooch

imagine the supper of sea bass, potato
he will grill for her.

The postulate morning

stands on tiptoe
wants to see past the fence
the brick wall
tall buildings with their
measure of privilege.

I have seen things stumble
before they fall
tiny hands hold a diligence
nobody protects.

In the spotlight of the moon
my mother divested her loss
sent it out to sea
along with her body

left behind her shadow
its tilted matrix
trickster seasons
that come and go
come and go
in a flash.

On Sundays

we scrub clean
the fingers of our children
shoplift the dirt under their nails
call them the *pearly face of God*
in a neck tie, patent shoes
sit them in a pew
quiet
sterile as a subdued Jesus.

But holiness doesn't always
wear pert robes
a hymn book.

You exit the pew
move out past the faded chapel
thick stands of spruce
twine your hair
into a rope save.

In August

the moon holds a soft face
won't tattoo the armchair with permanence
cast us down
turn the playground supplicate.

I cup a butterfly in my palm
marvel at the body of moths
purple chalk the pavement

want to become wind
the bright shooting star
ambassador of a green planet
beyond name calling.

You go around

in a rabbit suit sleeper
no one can pry loose.
It is the pale white of oatmeal
has flop ears, padded feet
a crush of fur, half dangle of stub tail.
At night sleep on your side peaceful
as if the moon, the sun converse
the dark and light marry.

And I want to protect what is yours
feed it apricots and honey
beet greens, a faultless moon.

You sleep in a skin of rabbit
tuck it over your head
have the pale skin of the day lily
closed eyes of the dreamer
can pass for a bunny in the field
petable creature
soft curd in a flan dish

every night invent stories
console the dead soldier
grow back the girl's severed arm
offer up golden apples to the giant
barges of bread
the tea marked *repentance*.

Happiness called

didn't boast chorizo pizza
a red mustang
my radiator still hissed
stock options were bought and sold
the economy waxed nimble.

I was being my clandestine self
the one who sips lemon fizz
stalks the forest in gum boots.
Apples thudded the ground
stones rose and fell
the dog listened. .

Happiness called
no hit record, ticket parade
led me into your hemisphere
where thistle sing
the dark dances
even on a knife blade.

The Houdini of Cramped Space

you conjure goats out of the rag pile
velvet a doll sled
parody want till it sings canary
set the table in festive plates.

All night your tiny book
whispers rhubarb pie
a waltzing bear beside the fish dock.

See how mice genuflect
the dark sky sizzles
the tired boy yawns
a bed rows in

empty milk jugs
get splashed with cream
from the moon's gold faucet.

It is auction time

in the county's warehouse.
Out comes the badger shaving brush
an ancient pram
panels of carved mahogany
the dented fire screen
black ice skates

out comes the painted rocking horse
metal dog pen, tent poles
tarnished spoons
a riding saddle, binoculars
the porcelain headed doll
with a droopy eye.

It feels like Christmas in August
folks bid
search for a bargain
as if things hold the promise
of a second life
beyond the original

as if everything waits
to be noticed
patient.

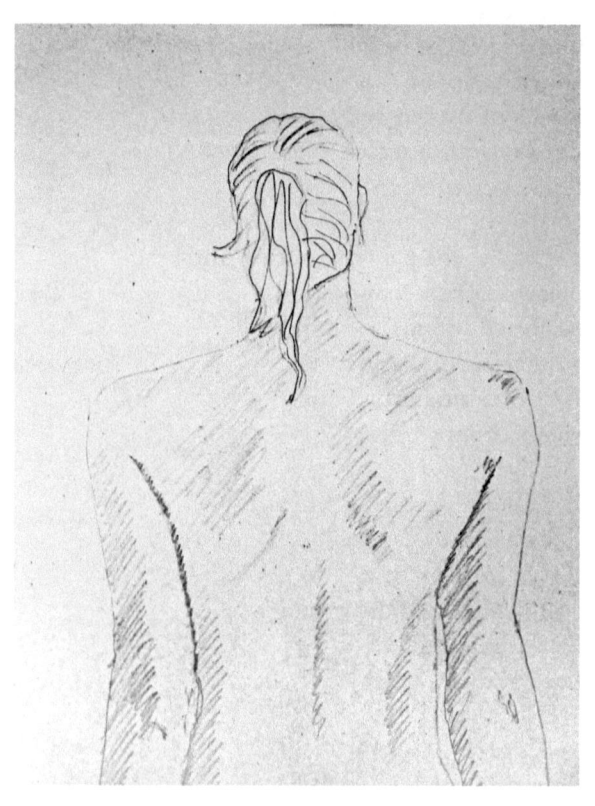

PART THREE

Windfall

There are seasons

that pander to no one
are parochial want
parading as last year's swimsuit.

I want to wake up
the apostle of snow
slide children over the hills
wrap couples in the wonder
of ice crystal.

There are seasons
that walk abroad on stilts.
These are the ones
that will ask the most.

You deal in rice and ringlets

loose circumstance
disarm me
no more stereophonic
bright Portia in a blonde wig
late night ice cream.

Call me forensic
the girl who cups flame
eats death out of a marriage
hoists up her children

wants to show you
how willing a soul can be
undeterred
brave.

We cracked the egg

sat it in our palm more decent
than the wreckage of ball fields
watched the shell wrinkle
splay into a web
peered in
ostrich, fledgling duck
bug born fantasy
who can tell what an egg will yield

called out for more
more eggs, more spoons, a new napkin.
The waiter wasn't happy
as if requests damn.

We cracked the egg
death by attrition
or built in from birth
did it behind the patterned napkin
but even modestly disrobed death
can feel squeamish
the betrayal of oyster, grilled fish
ask us to disguise
slop its globular body into a batter bowl
transform into cake.

Some years are broken toys

the rag rug embedded
with grape stain
food stamps
haul ass work
children waiting.

But one day
there will be a stranger
who offers up
more than a yellowed envelope
petals for the deceased

in whose eyes
the sun travels
the river empties.

You lean over my morning

see if it still breathes
are you there, my friend
offer up your willing
preternatural
a spin in the new wagon.

Is this all it takes
to unthread my future
turn the day from genocide?

You name nothing *terrible*
walk miles without your thirst crippling
till empty plates keep the memory
of beet and potato

as if over time
you have become offering
cup the ordinary things—
pitcher, river, bridge, plant, cat, shoes
in your own being
sheen them holy.

We are pouring syrup

raspberry, as it happens
will color our floats
flavor the past.

Some days are like this
you take the runt pup and soothe
lathe mayo onto your sandwich
dollop ice cream into a float glass
call it *feast*
as if every child needs a home
fried egg
cup of froth
pantomimes.

It is August and rainy
the love of slowness has not yet
been bred out.
Things come and go -
money, coats, chairs, work
kisses, houses
cramped rooms and big ones
the bright corsage, wilted rose
liquid sunset mated to stingy.

Sometimes it is hard to plaster the past
with a durable float
become the playground for grasshoppers.

Before wind generators

the aeronautics of space
ice boxes and creameries
sleazy bars and treacle
before our birth cradle
disposable diapers
lollypops and slush cones
the constellation of hope fastened
to a money lender

before house lots and fence line
slaughtered mustangs
the tree felling, frog eating
oil mongering
before mashed potatoes and gravy
eyelet stockings invaded by cancer
before heart failure
tooth replacement
four square houses with chemical lawns
a swing set

before I learned the name for *mama papa apple pickle toy*
before more complicated words set in -
parochial ectopic modernity embodiment
before I climbed the couch
delivered a soliloquy
broke someone's heart

a second coming was foretold

doesn't worry its brain
over camera-ready art, recession
the disproportionate allocation of wealth
doesn't need to sing for a meal
set up a neon sign
network

doesn't promise to breathe easy
deflect flames.

In some eyes is it possible that
even paradise on a shoestring
remains the bright corsage
of a burning bush?

We came slow

the light peeled and we allowed it
the days shrank and we allowed it
there were peridots large as marbles
baked potato casseroles
derelict shoes and kid glove ones
sheep
many sheep.

You drove out the cold
invested us with bright woolies
lunchboxes
after school crumpets, tea.

We came slow.
There was time.
No one knew the names yet for suffering
knew the stapled field
blue adagios
broken nose.

The day waxed perfect
even as it shrank.
Our ponies were bred to jump
over high fences
and they flew.

The whirligig couldn't hold us

nor our mothers
when tales of the selkies departed
and they grew thick as the land
less winsome.

We thought we were bigger
bigger than stairways
well-mannered dogs
that one day the prize card
would descend
red convertible our yard
turn our families happy.

The whirligig couldn't hold me
nor uncle's cigars
wild west stories

not even the cosmos
desperate for stargaze.

We couldn't stare you down

finally you grew an olive tree
in a matchless grove
and others came to worship
your alabaster roof
stands of nightshade

and still you grew larger
became linnet, courtyard
river and hill
became city
the wind that contains
the wind that abolishes

became names, guttural morning
the past vilified
moon infested
tart and tincture
hope

became mourning
our sumptuous
profane.

To praise the dark

takes memory making
erasure
the lost footing
matted swan song
meld of want
satiety
an empty room.

I have known times like this
when everything turns
more than preamble

pagan birds spiral
the asparagus sings
the sky tumbles
stars of crystal.

Who says we are impermeable

that the boy yanked
from his mother's arms
will forget
lovers ache for each other
then move on
families stay undimmed by the
burden of Chernobyl

who says we are darkened mirrors
on a grey plain
the night speaks only in metal

that girls who cling to the last
romance of their summer dresses
must die or turn blind?

I call you Inspector Caruso

for the dedicated way you peel
face masks
the blue tenement
till there is a quiver of light
fist of grain, potato
kisses and handholding

like the way you work diligent
leave room
aware that sometimes the night saves
a considerate hand is advisable.

You peel back the night
soft, slow
no shaved trees, scalped frogs
animals gone to the stock yard
mishandled hedge fund, chicanery.

See how the night turns luminous
holds up the moon, strangeness
our bodies become ant
pear tree, comet
star gaze.

Who calls the bird out of hiding

spins the imaginary ball
night maps the child
ensures the mother's arms
stay faithful

who vouchsafes the grape
calls longing out of its doze bed

pregnants the dark
so that risen over the sliced
fields of lavender
the ear of the moon
will listen?

Our neighbors are round and poor

let the lamplight lead
kiss the wings of pigeons
as they fly
offer up mouthfuls of okra, fry bread
as if it is feast table.

Are some of us wired like this
so generous love leaks a banquet
the torn house gets nursed back
colicky child learns soothe words
the melody of skin

are some people unnoticed galaxies
bright flames
inside an ordinary looking suitcase?

You speak in parables

pull toys nobody sees.
They are spotty, ice caked
a long road off a grey highway.

It can take years to find my way
not grope
invite the strange, mired
slow and fisted
bite sized and blue courtiers.

You speak in parables
deal in mismatched
almsgiving
the ice strangled tree
deal in more than pistol factories
home in a shoebox.

See how I caravan hope
crate apples
take the path by the river

make your worn down
ancient pasture
my home.

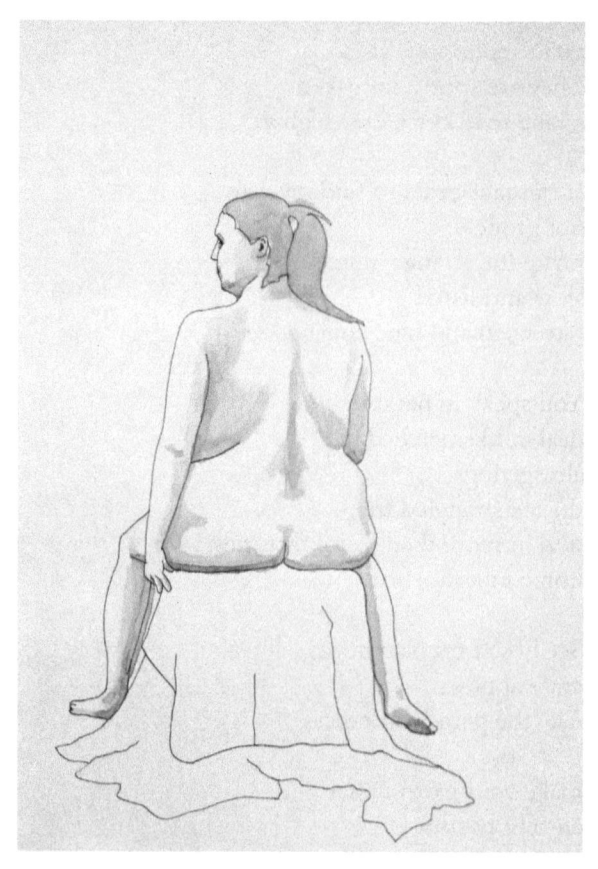

Part Four

We are Stargazing

The playground of the dark

won't stand on one foot
suck the salt out of the ocean
whip the soldier blind
parody sickness *just because*

won't turn the night fisted
profit the ordination of flox
collect tar pitch, gossip
the ordinary assaults on a hymn

won't congregate want
trophy elk
smash the doll's head
anarchy summer
make life into a glass eye
hooked fish, horsewhip

cups what we cast out
inside the sky's tutelage
till it shines.

When I tap terrestrial

out of my weakest keys
will you still come calling
not view me as derelict

the poster child for loss
in a trite world
the girl who eats spiked cake
then shrivels

will you believe
whatever is periled
can speak

silence grows its own
kind of handrail
not dim witted
but blessed?

We came here to play

brought our ball, birch sticks
sandwiches
butter beans, gherkin
sometimes even a slice of cake

erected ships, pup tents
a pig colony
spent hours setting up
our sand castle, moat

knew the night as more than
spilt ink, a scissored hem
reordered our mothers' lives
parents' marriages
till there was more
than cramped rooms
a valley of hiss fits.

We scoop up fantasy

the way some folks
shield from cancer
unencumber the grass
sew the world safe

scoop and scoop
till the wolf rescinds
the felled woodsman
turns phosphorous

slide into your shoes
slippery as fish
help the giant make amends
for his people eating.

We talk about bright wings

blouse factories
the thin boy who sells chickens
about paper flags made out of
the flanged light of winter
rice scattered about the streets
the wall clock that pushes
carved children out the door
then eats them.

I don't want it to end
don't want the world to crop us
make me into a circus
cramped town
don't want my words
to turn rock hard
ravenous.

I am fingering the fanciful

a trip to Soriano
the Carpathians
slabs of elfin bread
the rabbit infused meadow

my clotheslines of greed empty
my has been dress resurrected
as good blood.

Sometimes do we laugh
over nothing
while the world weeps?

I crumple paper

send you a note
no antidotal version of spring
just blue ink
a margin of blurred tulips.

See how the night traffics in
lost shoes, hairpins

the cargo trunk of a paper plane
can hold all the kisses of the world
in a single flight.

In the soft hollow

white thighs burn
bright candidates tango
lips trace the grass

the food is good
evening hosts the hushed vowels
of a pear tree
night animals protect

bread lifts
love carries no anvil.

This morning

news from the other world
comes flirty
wants strappy shoes, a tango
the man who waits table
wears his lips moist as a paintbrush.

No one is sick
forced to beg
work mind numbing repetitive
the bus driver sings *take all of me*
the silver haired woman
unbuttons her coat.

Swallows swoop then lift
your body shelters the meadow
I yank up my skirt
every pale eyed stranger
arrives with a kiss.

The bandoneon kept saying

play me your soul's weight my friend
and I will listen

Some things come without cost
are free tuition in a calculated world.

Blue accordion, Piazzolla
the moon's constituency
of marriage material.

Darling, we have come so far
amid the morning glory.
To play in this field is a
ceremony of birds.

We are playing Parcheesi

It is early October
a bundle of suitcases
borrowed room.

Some of us sleep fitful
are snoop ears, a soiled clothesline
anxious sinner in a slant dress.

It appears I will beat you
hands down with my words tied.
You will be forced to make dinner
spoil me on soup and toast
piled high with rocket

call it a feast table
as if it is not what might be
but what survives in us
that saves.

You want me to kiss and tell

tell the story of what
the so many nights

how the hours ran thin
the supper was uneventful

I dreamt
a one room bungalow
writing table, bed for two
white sand beach beside rock

dreamt
someone consonant
you.

The silhouette of the moon

reminds me of your face
stark naked
no mealy.
I like to travel it
take in the handholds
rest stops
matter of fact
kisses.

The world frightens me
its rock ledges
balance beams.

I string a bracelet
of tiny bells
run my finger across the
soft pulse of your forehead
angular nose
where birds nap
the sky pauses to star gaze

where love holds sway
holds sway.

We are peeling oranges

they are plump
come from far away
worth being prized
for their journey.

I like to go inside slow
slide open each cobbled road
honey hive
where the juice lives

flood you with orange
the sun licked river
till words float away
ones that won't ever be
enough to carry us.

We are peeling oranges
an ordinary afternoon
start of July
heat crazed day.

And has my life always been like this
a constellation of rivers
half bedraggled dress
kisses so sodden the birds weep
fish rise up from the river?

You have bride groomed for the day

but are not saying
some things wait for us
with a spotty veil
hold pine cone and cactus
the mud strewn path to the well.

And is it dangerous to talk thick
of your lamplight
tease it with pecans and piccolos
words so secret our lips ache?

All my life has been cluttered
with showgirls
a church pew
eyelet
widow's view
of the coast.

I took you home last night

fed you turnip
grilled beets, ginger
not that you expect things
come with a yardstick.

I like your body this way
always open
a picture book worth page turning
star struck planet

like the way you sing
my uncharted ocean
feather the sky in me.

You hold no peephole

over the moon
are no bestiary of cardboard boxes
locked rooms, a name plate

have racy hands
innuendo
folk tales
know how to calm dirty shed days
turn the crushed bud into orchid
ribbon my field.

Inside your hands' blue margin
I become unfolded dress
the half fish with the golden tail.

What if our bodies

are fluid lightning
so holy the birds curtsy
peonies grow double girth

what if I am traveling
a flint road
and to touch you
is to remember
how paradise feels
on a shoestring?

Kiss me then.
Let it stay precious
as the first.

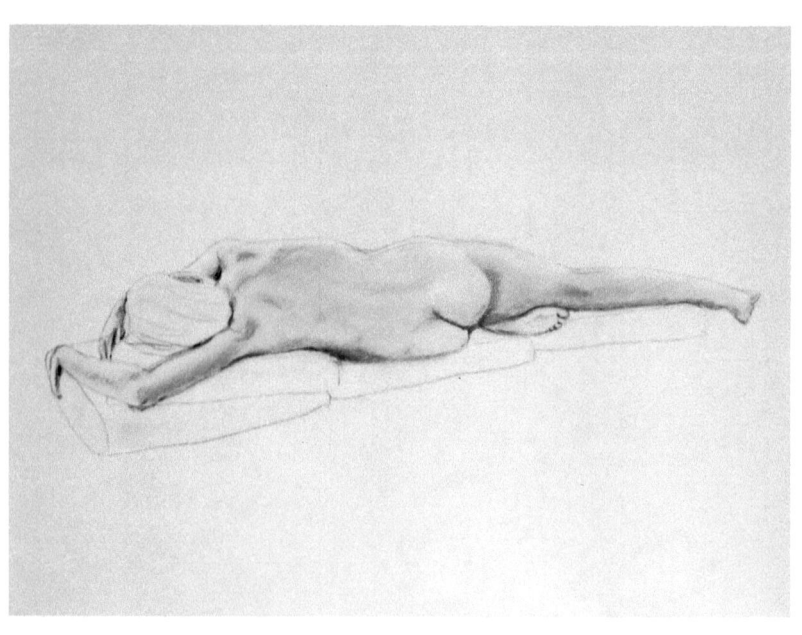

Part Five

Liquid Kisses

You wander my body

from forehead to toes
good navigation requires slow time
the plush of pliable limbs
a less trafficked road.

Folks make fun of
my muddied taffeta
how we sidle the dark
arm in arm
star gaze

but the body remembers
pets the past smooth

consecrates love
into a new map
of snow.

You are inventive

paper crane the past
set up our tea tray
blue eyelet
doll size cups

rabbit bites
lemon cake
kiss party
under the bed sheets.

Every day I let you wander

my shore
slide into my boots
romp through the sedge naked

let you nap and sing
snuggle up with me
under the faux sheepskin

bolt down wedges of good bread
Black Bomber cheese
gherkins

child happy
satiated.

Everything seduces me

the wind
dress collar of tulip
wish list of clover
my son's silken crop of hair
the sanctuary of fire escapes
the girl in tartan plaid
boarding the late train
for Scotland

and of course your eyes
that are peopled with trees
light up a shepherd's sky
call back the birds.

In the right light

when the pinnacles of want recede
the world holds no ice axe

I refind the child in me
that pale faced sweetness that holds
a silvered ocean
busted shells
lets the tide eddy.

She is rocking
rocking
rocking
no where to go
no place to be
but here.

It is the season

when love wears no stab wounds
you get what you see
loose hair
eyes liquid blue as the sky
more trustworthy.

It is hard to squire fate
tie your life to what vanishes
prospect the dance camp of roses

but fancy does as fancy sees
I unbutton my blouse
my hands
my heart
as if everything
grows thick as poppies
will last.

Some lovers stay with us

as seed carriers
wedding trousseaus
that never abort

become the bright cameo
inside our coat
first snow of winter

joy of so much happiness
forever stalled
on one kiss.

I vow by midnight

and dawn light
by the cat's tray table
the dog's kibble
by my children's bronzed fingers
the fleeting glory of lilac
by acrimony and loss
so much loss

I vow by my hips vagrancy
the pall mall version of swing set
vow by my *Yes Yes Yes*
to this valley of love
you.

It is good to remember

that even a small space
can squire singsong
a lack of ice
sparrows still descend
for a breadcrumb

good to remember
my mother is more than
her crushed voice
deathbed

amid February's snowfall
in the palm of my pocket
she plays.

It is early June

the sun a misfit in the sodden sky.
I have put the teapot to brew
want to do more than rehearse things
wear them provisional
the sly ambition
wedged inside chocolate

pour from the pot
place the cup between your fingers
let it offer up her warmth
aroma of petal

clear my voice
tell you what your love means
how it climbs the trellis
of my forgotten roses
stirs my soul
till we are ageless
dine with petulant angels
a liquid sunset

how in your body
my body finds a home.

On Bastille Day

the carrier pigeon sings
the neighbor in the house dress
pencils her eyebrows
children play hide and seek
the tea kettle steams
words upload to confetti
fireworks, flame

I pin my heart to my chest
woo you with Sappho
Piaf
let the sea have its sway.

You are eating kippers

in the Bristol bed and breakfast
ignore their glazed over eyes
delight in the oily
the fried tomato, hash browns
rack of toast.

I have known mornings like this
when we eat what was once alive
cut it into pieces, devour
don't care if it was a marriage
family, two children
a life.

It is late March.
Tulips punctuate the front lawn.
Light fingers the curtain.
I spoon oatmeal, sip coffee
flirt across the table
know your lips are flammable
will be exiled only till
the arrival of toothpaste.

That even more, my darling
it's your larger decency I am after -
and it sings
it sings.

In the thorn bush

a bird chirps
rants in her greenery

like the hours of my heart
that slide onto your branch
sip the sun, the moon
stargaze.

In the bright vestibule
wait sailors and kumquat
a girl in dark glasses

the cod fish sings
worship walks wider
than newspaper.

I could promise you

Savanna in winter
the girl who blondes the dark
as it flees
twin corgis
blue armed happiness on a stick
plastic tiger lilies
couple dolls that only kiss
when the sun turns maniacal

could offer you Pushkin
the lace lipped pram
best shop bread pudding
unpetulant sunrise

but then bee colonies collapse
the phenomenological turns quick sand
animals die caged
people drown

so what I can offer you
is this clear eyed traipse
through the sweetgrass
our so very fleeting beauty
my weeping willows
temporal psalm.

The day is heavy with the scent of sedge

I walk but my feet lift
trees nuzzle the flesh of sky
children shoot marbles
suck ice cones
dogs run off
are fetched back.

From here
the umbrellaed past
feels palpable
the orchard spills apples
the old man on the bench
recites a hymn
startled, my mother rises up
spot cleans her good dress
slips back into those
bird pecked heels.

You rattle the stars

sidle up to my vampish
till I am more than
disappointment
the raked field
shoes gone crooked

don't talk about
the cost of cauterizing
in a spotty world.

I watch you extract
dead fish
from the bowl
of my father's mouth
till he speaks
decent.

In the script of your world

I am not
just a fallen clause
blued Danube

flirt with the sun
wet mouth of hose
let the meadow borrow
my timothy
fireweed, bramble

meet you barefoot
in my ancient dress.

Summer roams.
Birds on a wire hoop
turn my hair into spangle.

I map my hands

with your secret eye
that sees through wallpaper
suets the bird feeder
suckles the field
mingles with jack rabbit
vole, children

map my hands
by your body's allegiance
your dwarf cake
ribbons of snow

map my voice by your
lack of imperialism
the way you leave room
always leave room

till names blur
our blood comingles
I am licked double
inside the silver flange
of your moon's trespass.

We sing morning star and hope

sing *feast — let there be feast*
sing peonies and lyric poetry
across the green gimlet fields

and festive kisses
swamp kisses
kisses for 2's and 3's and 4's

and forever moonlight
humming across the thorn bushes
the campfire
twined bodies

and merciful roses
ones that hold strong
past the first frost
their bright crimson
bolted to blaze.

I sew on wings

call them *missionary*
aerial landscape

call them *embryotic*
a scrap of my mother's dress
the dark with no dossier of blades.

See how the ground shakes
with confetti
dust surfaces glisten
our posed trajectories unhinge

my feet of clay
lift
into sky angels.

Toni Thomas lives in Portland, Oregon. Her poems have been published in Austria, Spain, New Zealand, Canada, England, Scotland, and Australia. In the United States her work has appeared in over fifty literary magazines including *Prairie Schooner, North Dakota Quarterly, Hayden's Ferry Review, the Minnesota Review, Notre Dame Review, Poetry East*, and more. She has been twice nominated for a Pushcart prize, and won several awards. She has published thirteen collections of poetry and three books for children.

Her figurative clay sculptures have been shown in gallery exhibits in Portland and Chicago, displayed in literary magazines, and housed in private collections in the U.S. and England.

Her short documentary *One of Us* was shown at the Trans-ideology: Nostalgia festival in Berlin and at the Museum of
Contemporary Art in Taipei.

Since Toni loves to create and sits buried in reams of poems, manuscripts, clay figures and images….she likes to imagine all of them out in the world, swaying wild as the lupine.

tonithomaspoetry.com

www.ingramcontent.com/pod-product-compliance
Lightning Source LLC
Chambersburg PA
CBHW021444080526
44588CB00009B/680